VISITORS ARRIVE UNCERTAIN. THEY LEAVE ENAMORED.

Visitors arrive uncertain. They leave enamored.

Le visiteur arrive hésitant, il repart séduit.

Los visitantes llegan perplejos. Parten enamorados.

Besucher kommen mit Zweifeln behaftet und gehen bezaubert vondannen.

Przybysze zjawiają się z wątpliwościami. Wyjeżdżają zachwyceni.

I turisti arrivano incerti. Se ne vanno affascinati.

Besøkende vet ikke hva som venter dem, men reiser sin vei betatt.

半信半疑だった観光客は、魅惑されて出て行く

Οι επισκέπτες φθάνουν διστακτικοί. Φεύγουν όμως καταγοητευμένοι

방문객은 불확실함속에 도착합니다. 돌아 갈때는 매혹되어 갑니다.

Chicago, USA
The Heart Of The
Midwest.

Illinois Native American

Photographer: David J. Maenza

Written by: Jay Flynn

Designed by: James Groll

Art Direction by: Paul Collins

Edited by: Bob Hale

Associate Editor: Jeanette Rawley

Black and white photos courtesy of Special Collections Department, Chicago Public Library

CITIES ARE LIVING THINGS.
CHICAGO'S BIRTH HIDES IN
LEGEND AND DIM HISTORY. LIKE
MANY CITIES IT TOOK ITS FIRST
HALTING STEPS, FALTERED AND
PICKED ITSELF UP AGAIN. CHICAGO
HAD AN UNRULY ADOLESCENCE
AND THEN IT DIED. FEW LIVING
THINGS RISE AGAIN, ESPECIALLY
WHEN STRUCK DOWN SO YOUNG.
CHICAGO DID. NOT CONTENT
TO REMAIN FORGOTTEN IN THE
PAST, CHICAGO WORKED TO
FULFILL A SEEMINGLY IMPOSSIBLE
FUTURE VISION.

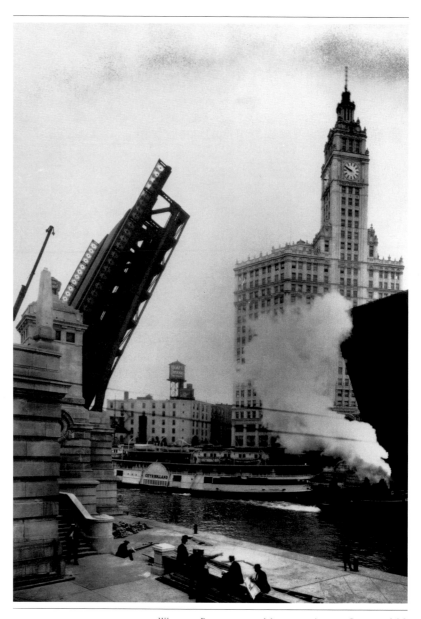

WRIGLEY BUILDING AND MICHIGAN AVENUE BRIDGE, 1900

CITY NEIGHBORHOOD, 1865

"BACK IN THE 1920'S, MY LATE FATHER USED
TO COMPETE AGAINST JOHNNY WEISSMULLER IN
CHICAGO RIVER MARATHON SWIMS."

NORMAN ROSS
RADIO PERSONALITY

The first people to settle along the green shores

of the glacier-carved lake were the Illinois native

Americans. Their name for the place near the

mouth of a slow river was Chicaugou. The name

encompasses nothing of the city's future

greatness. It means "wild onions" which grew

along the marshy shoreline.

Mecca for Immigrants, 1910

EUROPEANS FIRST HEARD OF CHICAGO FROM EXPLORERS AND MISSIONARIES LIKE JOLIET AND MARQUETTE. FORT DEARBORN WAS ESTABLISHED AT WHAT IS NOW THE CORNER OF MICHIGAN AVENUE AND WACKER DRIVE. THE FIRST PERMANENT EUROPEAN SETTLER WAS JEAN BAPTISTE POINT DU SABLE, A MAN OF FRANCO-AFRICAN DESCENT. DU SABLE CAME TO CHICAGO BECAUSE IT STOOD AT THE HEAD OF THE MAIN TRAILS TO THE UNSETTLED WEST. PROPHETICALLY, HE CAME HERE TO TRADE.

CULTURE COMES TO THE "HOG BUTCHER TO THE WORLD" -- THE ART INSTITUTE CA. !920

THE REBORN CITY GROWS: TURN- OF-THE-CENTURY PARADE ON SOUTH MICHIGAN AVENUE

Through the early and middle 1800's the city boomed. Grain flowed out on newly built railroads. Irish, Poles, Germans, fleeing starvation and tyranny in Europe, and newly-freed African-American slaves flooded the town and Chicago sprawled into a city. Then one searing October night in 1871, the city died.

Michigan Avenue south from Chicago Avenue

PLANNERS LIKE BURNHAM AND SULLIVAN SAW AN OPPORTUNITY TO REPLACE DISEASE-PLAGUED SPRAWL WITH A

MODEL CITY. URBS IN HORTO, A CITY IN A GARDEN BECAME THE MOTTO OF THE REBORN CHICAGO. ITS

CENTERPIECE WAS TO BE THE LAKE SHORE, NOT ACRES OF STONE.

THE LAKE SHORE WAS GIVEN OVER
TO ALMOST 25 MILES OF PARK AND
RECREATION LAND, CHICAGO'S
FRONT YARD. INSIDE THE CITY ITSELF,
560 PARKS TESTIFIED TO THE MOTTO.

STATE STREET BECOMES "THAT GREAT STREET", 1900

DARING ARCHITECTURE TOOK ROOT AND STRETCHED TO THE SKY. CHICAGO IS THE BIRTHPLACE OF THE FIRST SKYSCRAPER AND FIRST ELEVATED TRAIN LINE. TODAY, THE WORKS OF SULLIVAN, BURNHAM AND WRIGHT STAND BESIDE THOSE OF MODERN ARCHITECTS. MIES VAN DER ROHE MADE CHICAGO A PROVING GROUND OF GLEAMING DREAMS IN STEEL AND GLASS.

SEARS TOWER UNDER CONSTRUCTION, 1979

THE SEARS TOWER STANDS AS A MILESTONE TO THE MODERN ERA IN CHICAGO. FOR MANY YEARS THE

TALLEST BUILDING IN THE WORLD, THE SEARS TOWER STRETCHES FROM PRIMEVAL LIMESTONE BEDROCK TO

THE CLOUDS. IN ITS SUPERLATIVES IT REPRESENTS LEAPS OVER COUNTLESS STRUCTURAL OBSTACLES THAT

DAUNTED THOSE WITH SMALLER VISIONS.

THE SEARS TOWER LOOMS
1454 FEET ABOVE STREET
LEVEL. THREE STATES
CAN BE SEEN FROM
THE OBSERVATORY.

CHICAGO IS A LIVING MUSEUM OF ARCHITECTURE. WALKING TOURS

CRISS-CROSS THE CITY, SHOWING VISITORS EXPERIMENTS AND

ACHIEVEMENTS OF BOTH THE PAST AND PRESENT AS CONSTRUCTION

CRANES NURSE NEW CONSTRUCTION SKYWARD.

CHICAGOANS OFTEN PLAY A
GAME OF GUESSING WHAT A NEW
BUILDING WILL LOOK LIKE. A
CASTLE, A GEOMETRIC SPIRE OR
EVEN A WEDDING CAKE ARE SOME
OF THE SUGGESTIONS AS A NEW
IRON GRIDWORK TAKES SHAPE.
AS THE CITY GROWS, IT IS HARD
TO IMAGINE THAT IT WAS
NOTHING BUT ASHES ABOUT 130
YEARS AGO.

"HAVING TRAVELED ALL OVER THE WORLD, I KNOW OF NO OTHER CITY THAT TAKES
AS MUCH PRIDE IN ITSELF AS CHICAGO. THE VITALITY AND TALENT OF THE PEOPLE...
AND THE ENERGY, THE BEAUTY OF THIS CITY, JUST EXCITE ME. AND THE CLIMATE...
WELL, IT MAKES YOU STRONG."

BILL KURTIS,
AWARD-WINNING BROADCAST JOURNALIST

THE TREASURES OF THE PAST ARE
JUST AS FONDLY REVERED AS
NEW BUILDINGS ARE AWAITED.
THE HISTORIC WATER TOWER,
BUILT IN 1869, BEST SYMBOLIZES
WHAT THE CITY IS ABOUT. IT
WAS PART OF THE DRIVE TO
MODERNIZE THE BOOMING
FRONTIER TOWN AND IT
SURVIVED THE GREAT FIRE,
GIVING THE PEOPLE THE HOPE TO
REBUILD. TODAY IT STANDS AT
THE HEAD OF THE MAGNIFICENT
MILE ON MICHIGAN AVENUE.

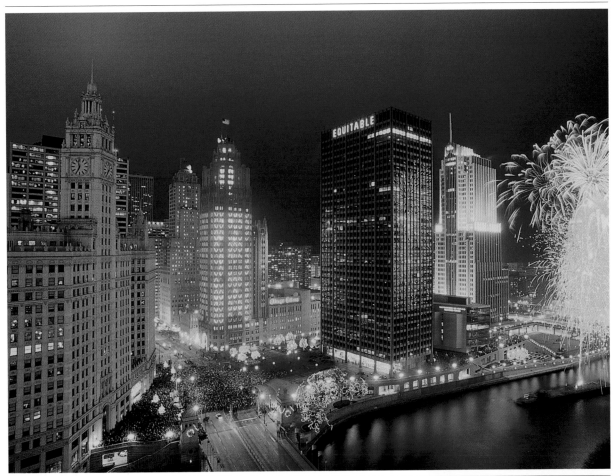

Marking the south end of the Magnificent Mile is the Wrigley Building. Named for the chewing gum magnate, it was built in stages and finished in 1924. The limestone and terra-cotta facade forms a gleaming backdrop to events on the Chicago river and the riverwalk, where people can stroll through a ribbon of parkland all the way to the lakefront.

Wrigley Building

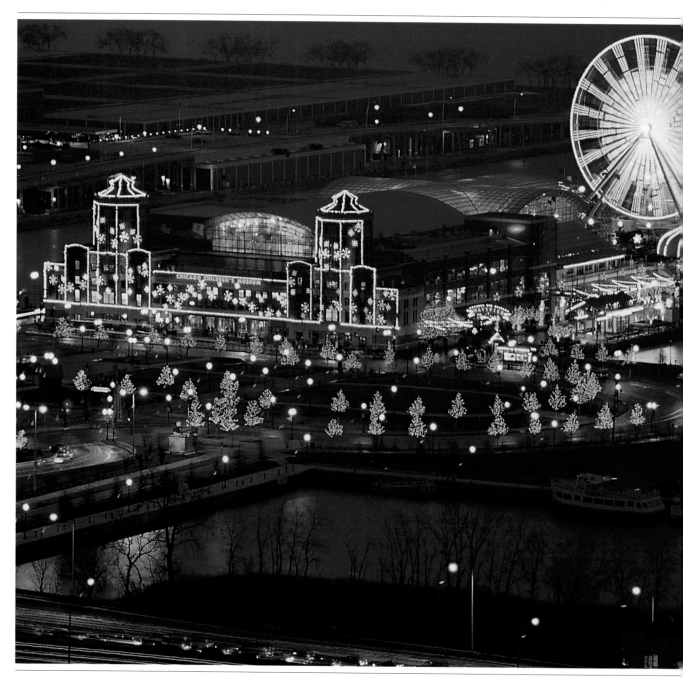

LIKE MOST HOMEOWNERS, CHICAGO KEEPS ITS FRONT YARD TIDY AND MAKES IT A SHOWCASE FOR THE CITY.

THE NECESSITIES OF WAR HAVE CREATED AND RECREATED NAVY PIER. HOWEVER , THE CITY WAS NOT

CONTENT TO ALLOW THE MILE-LONG BUILDING TO LANGUISH INTO DUST.

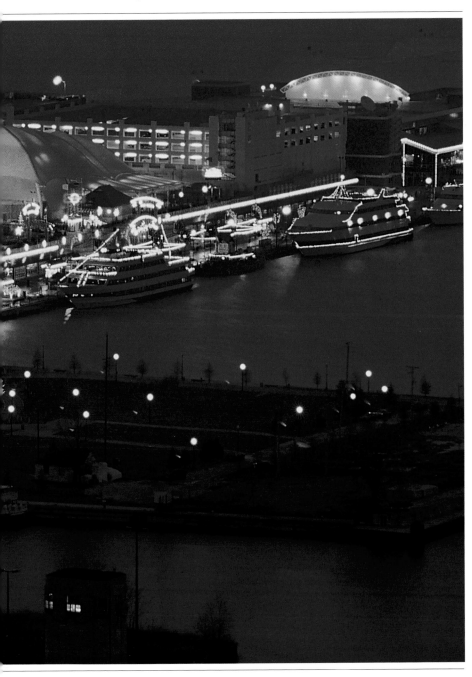

YEARS OF RECONSTRUCTION HAVE CREATED A FAMILY-FRIENDLY AMUSEMENT AND ENTERTAINMENT CENTER AT NAVY PIER. A SHORT CAB OR BUS RIDE FROM THE HEART OF THE CITY, IT OFFERS RESTAURANTS, DINNER LAKE CRUISES, RIDES AND CONCERTS. IT MAKES DOWNTOWN AS ATTRACTIVE AS ANY OTHER NEIGHBORHOOD.

THE REVITALIZED NAVY PIER BECOMES A WINTER PLAYGROUND

CHICAGO OFFERS CUISINE FROM EVERY CONTINENT TO SUIT EVERY TASTE.

OLDER NEIGHBORHOODS, ONCE
THE BASTIONS OF IMMIGRANTS,
DOT THE CITY. FOR ITS
INHABITANTS, CHICAGO IS A
CITY OF NEIGHBORHOODS. EACH
NEIGHBORHOOD HAS ITS OWN
ETHNIC PARADES AND FESTIVALS.
ST. PATRICK'S DAY FINDS EVEN
THE RIVER DYED GREEN AND THE
MAYOR LEADING THE PARADE
THROUGH THE CENTER OF THE
CITY. THE SNAP OF FIRE-
CRACKERS GREETS CHINESE NEW
YEAR IN CHINATOWN NEAR
WENTWORTH AND CERMAK.
CINCO DE MAYO, POLISH
CONSTITUTION DAY,
OKTOBERFEST, BUD BILLIKEN
DAY, FESTA ITALIANA - THE LIST
IS ENDLESS.

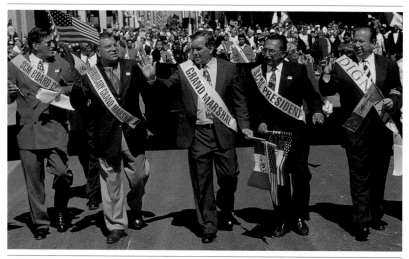

A BUSY MAYOR LEADS ONE OF MANY ETHNIC PARADES.

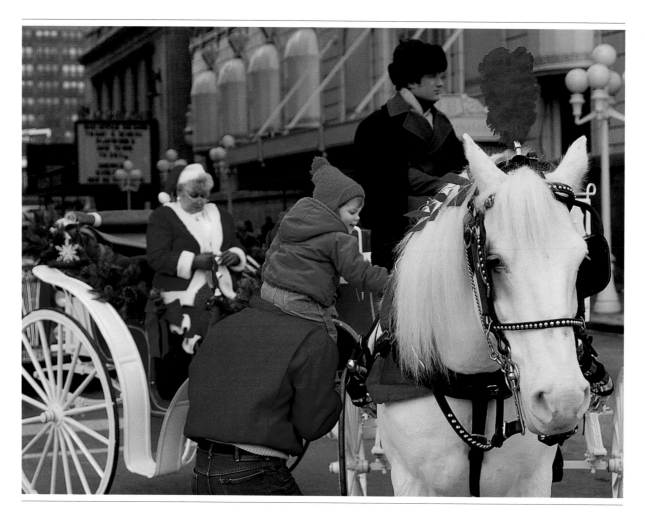

THE HEART OF THE CITY IS NOT JUST STERILE STEEL AND GLASS. IT IS A

CONSTANT CELEBRATION OF THE SOUL OF THE CITY - PEOPLE.

PARADES, FESTIVALS AND MUSIC ARE ALL PART OF DAILY LIFE IN THE

FINANCIAL AND BUSINESS DISTRICTS OF THE "LOOP". EVEN AFTER

BUSINESS HOURS AND ON WEEKENDS PEOPLE STAY DOWNTOWN FOR

THEATERS, RESTAURANTS AND EVEN A RIDE IN A HORSE-DRAWN

CARRIAGE.

FIESTA ON STATE STREET

Visitors also find the Chicago spirit is contagious and far-reaching. Businesses around the world are eager to share in it. Name a business or field and it probably has its convention in Chicago. Travel, sports, consumer electronics, medicine, film, autos, boats, dogs, cats, antiques are all reasons why Chicago greets more people than already live here as business visitors each year.

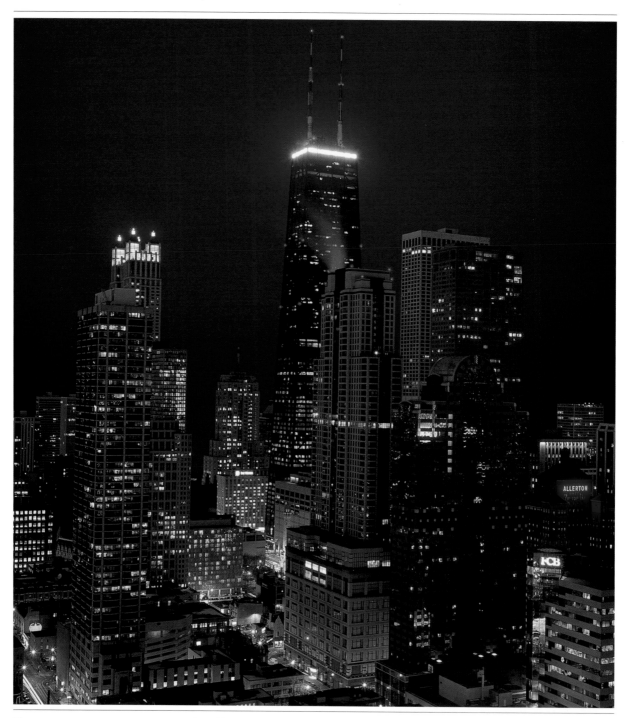

The crown of light at the top of the John Hancock Building can be seen from three states.

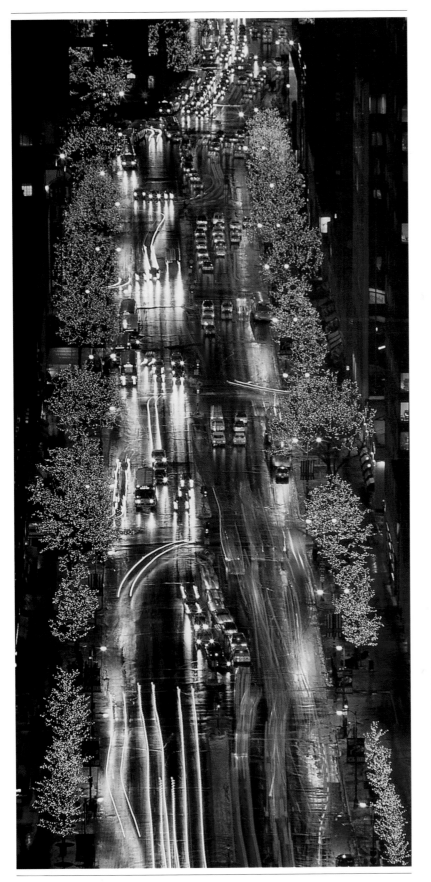

THE MAGNIFICENT MILE.

CHICAGO'S PREMIER REAL

ESTATE BECOMES A GLITTERING

ORNAMENT FOR THE WINTER

HOLIDAYS. THE DISPLAY OF

LIGHT STRETCHES FROM THE

RIVER TO LAKE SHORE DRIVE.

A BUSINESS AND HOTEL

DISTRICT, NORTH MICHIGAN

AVENUE ALSO BOASTS PREMIER

STORES FROM AROUND THE

WORLD.

WINTER CAN MEAN COLD,
WIND AND GLOOM. NOT TO
CHICAGOANS. IT MEANS HOT
CHOCOLATE, ICE SKATING,
TOBOGGANING AND CROSS-
COUNTRY SKIING. FUN IN THE
SNOW AT ALMOST ANY CITY
PARK GIVES YOU PLENTY OF
EXCUSES TO GET OUTDOORS TO
TRY TO CATCH SNOWFLAKES
ON YOUR TONGUE.

The Emerald City: Chicago in winter from Lincoln Park Lagoon

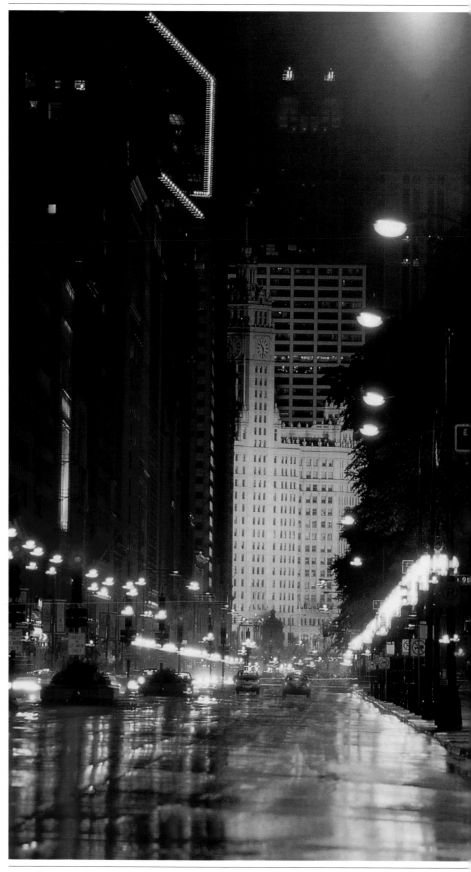

"They don't call it the Windy City for nothing. But if you don't like the weather in Chicago, just wait a minute. It'll change."

Unknown

Photo of the Wrigley Building from Roosevelt Road and South Michigan avenue, 1998

ALL SUMMER LONG THE PETRILLO BAND SHELL IN GRANT PARK ECHOES, THUNDERS, AND DANCES TO MUSIC

OF EVERY TASTE. YOU CAN SIT UNDER THE STARS AND LET THE MUSIC FLOW LIKE A COOL LAKE BREEZE.

EVERYONE COMES DOWN TO THE LAKEFRONT AND CELEBRATES ON THE FOURTH OF JULY WITH FIREWORKS,

FOOD AND, OF COURSE, JAZZ.

"WHEN I LEAVE THIS CITY, WHEN I
LEAVE THIS EARTH, THE ONE THING
I'LL KNOW IS THIS: I LIVED IN A CITY
THAT TRULY LOVED ME, AND I'VE
LOVED THEM."

MICHAEL JORDAN

"I LOVE PHOTOGRAPHING THE CITY AT NIGHT. IT IS LIKE OPENING A CHEST HEAPED WITH TREASURE. DAZZLING!"

DAVID MAENZA

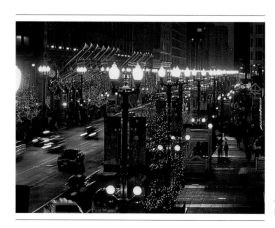

STATE STREET STORES TRY TO OUT-DECORATE
EACH OTHER AT CHRISTMAS

"Hog Butcher for the World,
Toolmaker, Stacker of Wheat,
Player with Railroads and the
Nation's Freight Handler;
Stormy, husky, brawling
City of the Big Shoulders:..."

Carl Sandburg
Poet

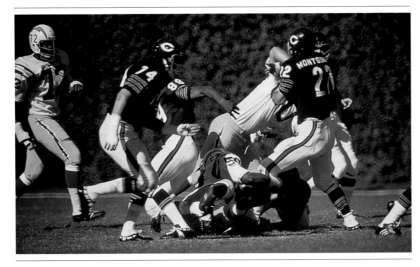

The early days of the National Football League: The Chicago Bears played at Wrigley Field.

North Michigan Avenue: Modern Skyscrapers reach past the historic Water Tower like fingers to the sky.

Lakefront Joggers enjoy the sunrise in front of the newly redesigned Adler Planetarium .

"THERE CAN BE NO BETTER PLACE THAN THIS.
THERE JUST CAN'T."

LORI GARZA -
EXPORT COORDINATOR

GATEWAY TO THE SUBURBS: NORTHWESTERN TRAIN STATION

"Chicago is beautiful.
Pictures don't lie."

Kimberly Gow
University student

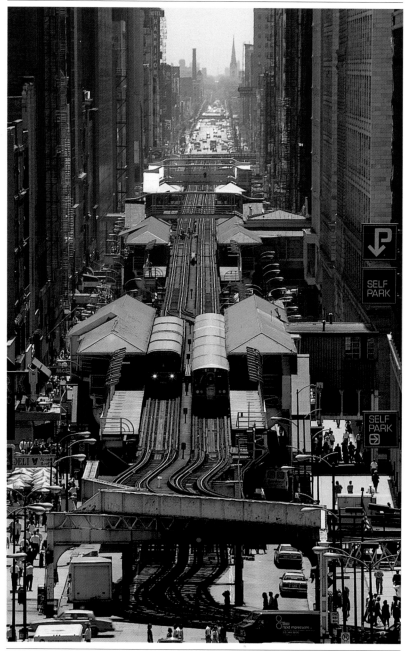

A CIRCLE OF ELEVATED TRAIN LINES FORMS THE FAMOUS LOOP THAT

CONNECTS WITH A MODERN TRANSPORTATION SYSTEM REACHING ALL

PARTS OF THE CITY AND SUBURBS INCLUDING TWO MAJOR AIRPORTS.

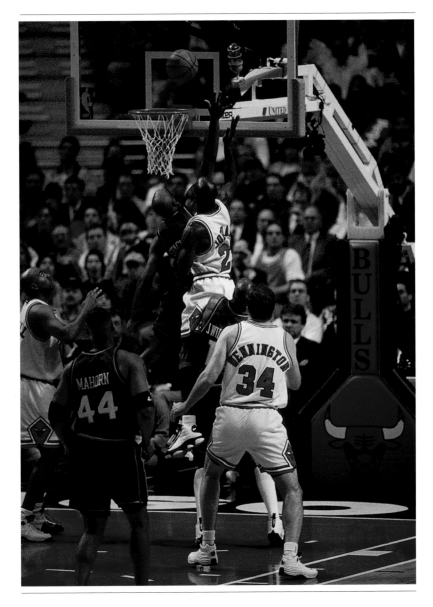

PROFESSIONAL TEAMS IN EVERY MAJOR SPORT EXCITE FANS IN MODERN VENUES THROUGHOUT THE CITY. THE CHICAGO BEARS DO BATTLE ON THE GRID-IRON AT SOLDIER FIELD. THE CHICAGO BULLS BASKETBALL TEAM SHARES THE UNITED CENTER WITH HOCKEY'S CHICAGO BLACKHAWKS.

CHICAGO LOVES THE NATIONAL PASTIME SO MUCH THAT ONE BASEBALL TEAM IS NOT ENOUGH.

THE CHICAGO CUBS AND WHITE SOX PLAY DAY AND NIGHT GAMES THROUGHOUT THE SUMMER.

BOTH BALLPARKS ARE LOCATED MINUTES AWAY BY ELEVATED TRAIN OR BUS FROM THE LOOP.

DEDICATED FANS ARE NOT JUST

SPECTATORS, THEY ARE PART OF

THE SHOW AT WRIGLEY FIELD

AND COMISKEY PARK.

"ALRIGHT NOW, LET ME HEAR YA"!

THANKS, HARRY

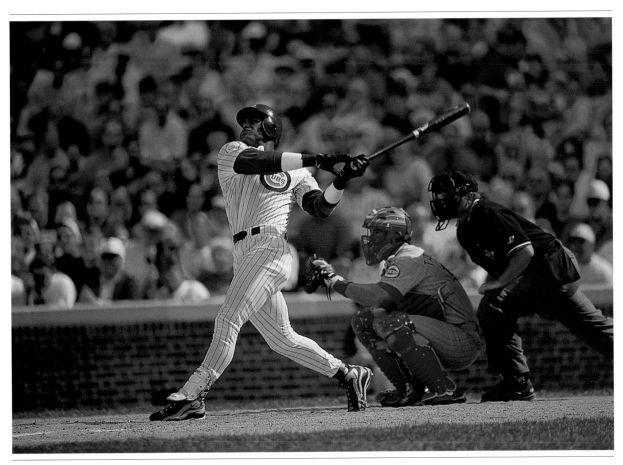

SAMMY SOSA HITS NUMBER 56 ON HIS WAY TO A RECORD 66 HOME RUNS. "CHICAGO, I LOVE YOU."

"FROM THE TOP OF THE SEARS TOWER, ONE MIGHT BELIEVE THE STREETS ARE PAVED WITH GOLD."

PAUL COLLINS
DESIGNER

THE FIELD MUSEUM of NATURAL HISTORY
IS A CENTER OF ON-GOING RESEARCH INTO
DINOSAURS AND PREHISTORIC MAN.

CHICAGO'S HEART PULSES TO

THE BEAT OF MUSIC. BLUES,

GOSPEL, JAZZ, CLASSICAL AND

OPERA. ONE OF THE

BIRTHPLACES OF THE FABLED

ART, CHICAGO BOASTS BLUES

VENUES WITH STAR PERFORMERS

SIDE BY SIDE WITH UP-AND-

COMING MUSICIANS.

THE LYRIC OPERA AND

CHICAGO SYMPHONY

ORCHESTRA ARE HOMES TO

A WIDE RANGE OF TALENTED

ARTISTS. MUSIC FESTIVALS

FOR EVERY TASTE SPAN THE

ENTIRE YEAR.

~CHICAGO WRITES ITS OWN MUSIC. IT MOVES
TO ITS OWN BEAT AND GETS INTO YOUR
SOUL.~

BOB HALE
CHICAGO BROADCASTER

ALL FORMS OF ART FIND A HOME HERE. THE ART INSTITUTE BOASTS A PRICELESS COLLECTION OF WORK OF

THE FRENCH IMPRESSIONISTS INCLUDING RENOIR, MONET, AND VAN GOGH. EVEN THE CITY STREETS ADD TO

THE COLLECTION. ON ANY GIVEN DAY, THOUSANDS PASS THE WORKS OF CHAGALL, MIRO AND PICASSO.

"MONUMENT WITH STANDING BEAST"

BY JEAN DUBUFFET
AT STATE OF ILLINOIS BUILDING

THE CHICAGO OF STONE AND
STEEL WILL NOT REMAIN FIXED
FOREVER. THE SEEDS OF THE
CITY'S FUTURE ARE SOWN
EVERYDAY. THE SKYLINE SEEMS
TO CHANGE MONTHLY AS
CONSTRUCTION CRANES
PIROUETTE TO A CONSTANT,
DRIVING THEME. DARING
DESIGNS ARC TO THE CLOUDS
AND ARE FILLED WITH PEOPLE
WITH NEW IDEAS AND VISIONS.

"I LOVE SEEING CHICAGO CHANGE TO MORE
BEAUTIFUL ARCHITECTURE EACH VISIT."

DANIEL BEEDERMAN
ATTORNEY

Four major marinas, serving both
power and sailing craft, line
Chicago's Lakefront

A lucky couple may even have
Lake Michigan all to themselves.

THE LAKE WILL REMAIN.

THROUGH A MIRACLE OF

ENGINEERING AND THE

DEVOTION OF THE CITY, THE

LAKE STAYS PRISTINE CLEAN,

TOUCHED ONLY BY THE BOATS

WHO SAIL IT AND SWIMMERS WHO

COOL OFF IN IT.

"CHICAGO HAS ALL THE ADVANTAGES OF A
BIG CITY AND ALL THE CHARM OF A SMALL
TOWN. THAT IS THE BEST OF BOTH WORLDS,
AND THIS IS THE BEST OF ALL CITIES."

JOAN ESPOSITO
TV NEWSPERSON

MARINA CITY

Lake Michigan: Pristine waters for swimming and boating

And there will always be the parks and the design of a city in a garden. They will improve and change to fit new lifestyles and peoples.

"I've been traveling the world since the early sixties when the only thing people thought about Chicago was "Al Capone Land". Now, it's not unusual to hear first-time visitors refer to Chicago as "that wonderful city by the lake". And why shouldn't they? Ours is truly a wonderful and proud city - it is very clean with a fabulous lakefront, numerous beautifully sculpted parks and distinctive architecture.

"We have a thriving business center, world-class restaurants and most of all, a diverse cultural community with first rate museums, the Chicago Symphony Orchestra, the Lyric Opera, an ever-growing theatre community and world class dance companies...and I haven't even gotten to our music scene, including our much envied jazz and blues clubs.

"We are not without our problems - what major cities these days are? But the difference is that we have the courage to confront our problems and strive to work them out. We are the finest example today of great ideas and great people. We call it...Chicagoland!"

Ramsey E. Lewis Jr.

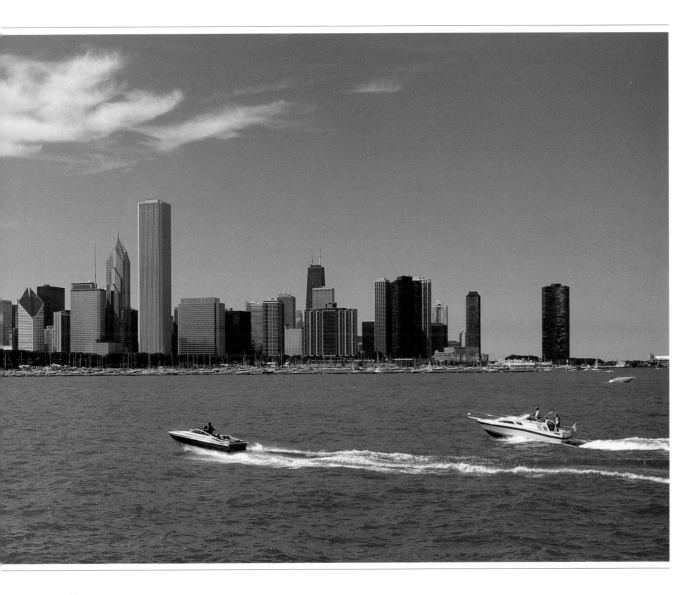

CHICAGO WILL REMAIN DEDICATED TO PEOPLE.

THOSE WHO LIVE HERE AND THOSE WHO VISIT WILL

STILL BE ABLE TO PLAY OR WORK HERE; TO FIND

HEART-POUNDING EXCITEMENT OR QUIET SOLITUDE.

ROMANTIC WALK: THE "GOLDEN COLLAR" NEAR LAKE SHORE DRIVE.

The Heart of the City: Buckingham Fountain in Grant Park

THE PEOPLE ARE THE FUTURE. THEY WILL CHANGE; NEW VISITORS AND CITY-

DWELLERS WILL ARRIVE. THEY WILL LEAVE THEIR MARK IN SOME WAY THAT

WILL BECOME INEVITABLY CHICAGOAN. IN EXCHANGE THE "I WILL" SPIRIT

WILL GROW INTO EVERYTHING THEY DO OR DREAM.

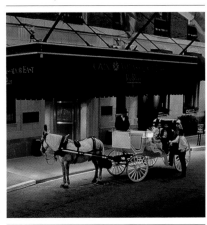

ECHOES OF YESTERDAY

"It looks like my wife."

JACK VON BURING
CONSTRUCTION COMPANY OWNER
WORMS, GERMANY

"Beautiful? I do not know. It is like a
fountain of steel."

SILVIA MENDOZA
CANDLEMAKER
MEXICO CITY

"Picasso, Miro, Chagall.... Chicago is
a museum of art! The whole city!"

PENELOPE MEVRELOS
NURSE
ATHENS, GREECE

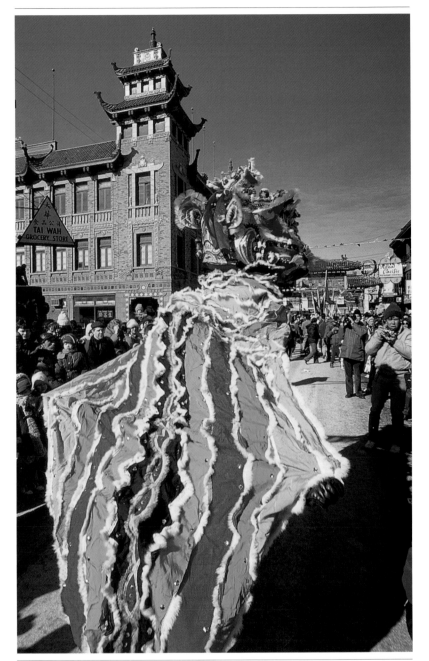

"THE FIRECRACKERS! THE FOOD! I AM SO HAPPY WE WERE HERE FOR
CHINESE NEW YEAR IN CHINATOWN. ONLY SHANGHAI WOULD BE BETTER."

JAMES DEGUZMAN
FARMER
THE PHILIPPINES

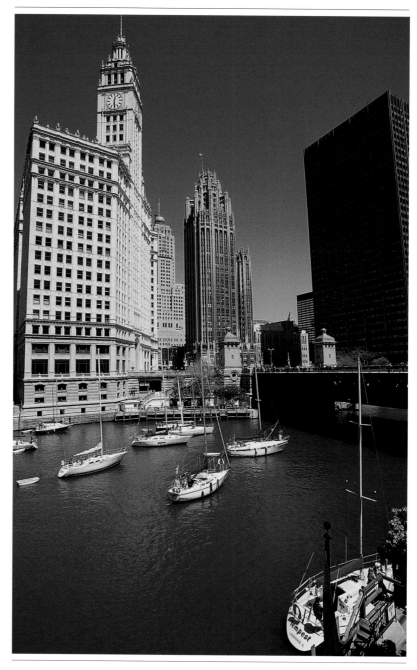

MICHIGAN AVENUE BRIDGE OVER THE CHICAGO RIVER

"IT'S LIKE A PILGRIMAGE. WE WAIT FOR THAT FIRST GREAT
DAY IN THE SPRING AND TAKE OUR BOATS TO THE BEAUTIFUL
LAKE. WHEN THE LAST BRIDGE GOES UP, WE'RE SET FREE."

DR. HAROLD ARAI
DENTIST
PARK RIDGE

BURNHAM HARBOR AT SUNSET

"CHICAGO IS SO MANY THINGS. IT IS
A HARBOR, A PARK, BIG BUILDINGS ....
AND HOT-DOGS!"

GEORG GARKUS
CAB DRIVER
RUSSIA

"It reminds me of the crown jewels in the tower of London. It sparkles and dazzles. Diamonds, rubies and emeralds laid out at your feet."

Franklin King
Boxing Promoter
London

"It is so hard to imagine what has happened here. Nothing but marshes and grass, then came settlers with tents and shacks. And then the Fire. I wish the people standing in the ashes could see this.... who knows? Somehow maybe they did. And that is why the city's here."

Benjamin Miles
Cowboy
Minot, North Dakota

Merchandise Mart

Museum of Science and Industry

"I have to come back four more times. First time I saw just the museums. There is so much in just one of them."

Charles Farina
Boat Captain
Sardinia

"Why do they make the river green and who was this Saint Patrick?"

Dr. J. Harrani
Maldives

"The bridges are amazing! They all swing up like swans raising their necks to salute the boats."

Martha Thylin
Pharmacist
Stockholm

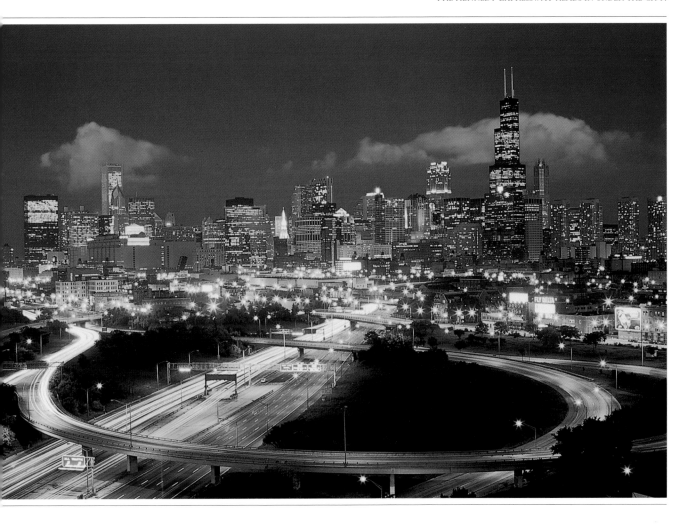

"Close your eyes and feel the city."

Lori Poppa
Accountant
Chicago

"Chicago wants you here. They want you to come. They have so many easy ways into the city. There are no walls, just the lights to guide you into its heart."

Franklin Feinberg
Investor
Tel Aviv, Israel

"Everything is so well planned and laid out. It is so convenient. All the planning of the last century has made a difference."

Erika Eddie
Property Manager
Lucerne, Switzerland

"THERE IS ONE THING ABOUT CHICAGO THAT IS CONSTANT. CHANGE. THE CITY
SEEMS ALWAYS EAGER TO GROW AND OUTDO ITSELF. RESTLESS, IT GREETS THE
DAWN EVERYDAY WITH ITS EYES LOOKING UPWARD. BIGGER, BETTER, FASTER. IT
SEEMS SOMETIMES THE ENERGY SPILLS OVER INTO THE ELECTRICAL STORMS THAT
LIGHT UP THE SKY HERE. IN THE SONG THE CITY IS CALLED "TODDLING". CHILDREN
TODDLE. CHICAGO IS A LARGE ZESTY YOUTH. ITS TODDLING DAYS ARE OVER."

MARYLIN MOONEY
UNITED KINGDOM

"IN ONE WORD.... BOOM! LIKE A ROCKET. THAT'S WHAT I THINK OF CHICAGO."

JOHN LEEMAN
FISHERMAN
NOVA SCOTIA

OAK STREET BEACH

"I WAS SURPRISED YOU COULD SWIM HERE.
NOT A HUNDRED METERS FROM A HUGE CITY
AND I STAND IN PURE, CLEAN WATER."

VINCENT FARCHIE
SOCCER PLAYER
BOLOGNA, ITALY

SHEDD AQUARIUM

"AT THE SHEDD AQUARIUM, THEY HAVE A
FOREST ... INSIDE A BUILDING! IT IS BRILLIANT,
JUST HOW IT BLENDS RIGHT INTO THE VIEW
OF THE LAKE."

MICHAEL BARTLEY
JAVELIN THROWER
CLIFFS OF MOHR, IRELAND

VIEW INTO THE "LOOP" FROM THE NORTH

"BELLISIMO! WHAT DOES THAT MEAN? IT
MEANS I LOVE DOING BUSINESS HERE. IT
MEANS I AM COMING BACK! DEFINITELY!"

ANTONIO LAZZARI
ROME